D1306492

DATE DUE

DRUGS

INHALANTS
A MyReportLinks.com Book

David Aretha

MyReportLinks.com Books

an imprint of

Enslow Publishers, Inc.

Box 398, 40 Industrial Road
Berkeley Heights, NJ 07922
USA

MyReportLinks.com Books, an imprint of Enslow Publishers, Inc. MyReportLinks®
is a registered trademark of Enslow Publishers, Inc.

Library of Congress Cataloging-in-Publication Data

Aretha, David.
  Inhalants / David Aretha.
    p. cm. — (Drugs)
  Includes bibliographical references and index.
  ISBN 0-7660-5280-X
  1. Solvent abuse—Juvenile literature. 2. Solvent abuse—Health aspects—Juvenile literature.
3. Substance abuse—Prevention—Juvenile literature. I. Title. II. Drugs (Berkeley Heights, N.J.)
  RC568.S64A74 2005
  362.29'9—dc22
                            2004002052

Printed in the United States of America

10 9 8 7 6 5 4 3 2 1

To Our Readers:
Through the purchase of this book, you and your library gain access to the Report Links that specifically back up this book.

The Publisher will provide access to the Report Links that back up this book and will keep these Report Links up to date on **www.myreportlinks.com** for five years from the book's first publication date.

We have done our best to make sure all Internet addresses in this book were active and appropriate when we went to press. However, the author and the Publisher have no control over, and assume no liability for, the material available on those Internet sites or on other Web sites they may link to.

The usage of the MyReportLinks.com Books Web site is subject to the terms and conditions stated on the Usage Policy Statement on **www.myreportlinks.com**.

A password may be required to access the Report Links that back up this book. The password is found on the bottom of page 4 of this book.

Any comments or suggestions can be sent by e-mail to comments@myreportlinks.com or to the address on the back cover.

Photo Credits: AP/Wide World Photos, p. 17; © 1994–2004, University of Washington, p. 18; © 2004 Partnership for a Drug-Free America, p. 27; © Corel Corporation, p. 9 (make-up bottle); Hemera Photo-Objects, pp. 3 (markers), 9 (spray can, tube, rubber cement), 33, 35; MyReportLinks.com Books, p. 4; National Archives, pp. 15, 41; National Institute on Drug Abuse, pp. 23, 37; Photos.com, pp. 3 (glue and spray can), 11, 21, 28, 39, 42; Stockbyte: Sensitive Issues, p. 34; U.S. Department of Health and Human Services, pp. 12, 29.

Cover Photo: Hemera Photo-Objects, (person's face, gas can in background, assorted bottles), Photos.com (gasoline can on top, spray can in background).

Disclaimer: While the stories of abuse in this book are real, many of the names have been changed.

MyReportLinks.com Books
Great Books, Great Links, Great for Research!

The Internet sites listed on the next four pages can save you hours of research time. These Internet sites—we call them "Report Links"—are constantly changing, but we keep them up to date on our Web site.

Give it a try! Type http://www.myreportlinks.com into your browser, click on the series title, then the book title, and scroll down to the Report Links listed for this book.

The Report Links will bring you to great source documents, photographs, and illustrations. MyReportLinks.com Books save you time, feature Report Links that are kept up to date, and make report writing easier than ever!

Please see "To Our Readers" on the copyright page for important information about this book, the MyReportLinks.com Web site, and the Report Links that back up this book.

Please enter **DRI1488** if asked for a password.

Report Links

The Internet sites described below can be accessed at
http://www.myreportlinks.com

▶**ONDCP Fact Sheet: Inhalants**   *EDITOR'S CHOICE
Information is provided on the background, effects, frequence of use,
and names of some of the more commonly abused commercial inhalant
products. Consequences of use, legislation, and statistics on treatment are
also included.

▶**National Inhalant Prevention Coalition**   *EDITOR'S CHOICE
Learn about the NIPC, an organization that promotes awareness of the
effects of inhalants. It also designs prevention campaigns, provides
training and technical assistance, and works with schools, the media,
Poison Control Centers, and many other groups throughout the country.

▶**Neuroscience for Kids: Inhalants**   *EDITOR'S CHOICE
This article lists a number of common household inhalants that kids sniff
or huff. Inhalants affect the body and nervous system, causing a variety of
sensory, motor, psychological, and emotional problems. Learn more about
the dangers.

▶**Tips for Teens: The Truth About Inhalants**   *EDITOR'S CHOICE
The tips provided at this Web site clear up some myths concerning
inhalants. Also learn about the risks and effects of using these products
as drugs.

▶**Inhalant Abuse Among Young People**   *EDITOR'S CHOICE
Statistical charts and graphs show the patterns of inhalant use and
attitudes among American schoolchildren. Information is broken down by
type of inhalant used, age, ethnicity, and gender.

▶**The Brain's Response to Inhalants**   *EDITOR'S CHOICE
Scientists report that inhalant vapors are stored in the tissue long after
they enter the body. Learn what inhalants do to your brain and nervous
system. Follow the links at the bottom of the Web pages to read more.

Report Links

The Internet sites described below can be accessed at http://www.myreportlinks.com

▶**Adolescent Admissions Involving Inhalants**

At this Web site, you will find government statistics on the race and ethnicity of adolescents who have used inhalants, as well as the age when inhalants were first used by the respondents. Includes charts and graphs.

▶**BodyFX: Inhalants**

Written for girls, this Web site explains the affects that inhalants have on different parts of the body, including the brain, nervous system, lungs, nose and ears, muscles, kidneys, and liver.

▶**Drug Facts: Inhalants**

Information is provided on the extent of inhalant use, its affects on health, treatment options for abusers, legal consequences, and street terms. Legislation that has made inhalant abuse illegal is also included.

▶**Drug Listings: Inhalants**

Abusing inhalants has short- and long-term affects on your body. Learn what they are and how regular use of these chemicals cause people to become tolerant and develop a dependence. Read more about who uses inhalants.

▶**eMedicine: Inhalants**

This report offers information on many aspects of inhalant abuse, including the effects, signs, history, treatment, medication, use patterns, trends, and more. A picture of a huffer is also included.

▶**Factline on Inhalants**

Many aspects of inhalant use are covered at this Web site, including legal issues, patterns of use, what parents and teachers should watch out for, the effects of inhalant intoxication, common inhalants, and warning signs of use.

▶**Fast Facts: Inhalants**

This summary provides an overview of the most important aspects of inhalant abuse. Read about the common types of inhalants used as well as the signs and consequences of using these dangerous chemicals.

▶**Freevibe.com: Inhalants**

The products abused as inhalants may seem like safe household goods, but they are actually very dangerous chemicals. Get the facts on inhalants, and learn the signs of abuse.

Any comments? Contact us: **comments@myreportlinks.com**

Report Links

The Internet sites described below can be accessed at http://www.myreportlinks.com

▶Inhalant Abuse

This Web site provides scientific information that will help you understand the risks involved with abusing inhalants. Learn what the risks are, why people use inhalants, the scope of abuse, the health consequences, and the patterns of inhalant abuse.

▶Inhalant.org

The Alliance for Consumer Education (ACE) promotes the safety, health, and well-being of children, families, and communities wherever household and institutional chemical products are used. In particular, its focus is on the prevention of inhalant abuse.

▶Inhalants

Find out why many young people abuse inhalants and some of the short- and long-term effects they experience. Would you know what to do if someone had an adverse reaction while using inhalants? Learn what to do in an emergency.

▶Inhalants: A Household Danger

The three main types of inhalants are organic solvents, nitrites, and nitrous oxides. All are abused in different ways. Learn more about the dangers of inhalants and the signs of abuse.

▶Inhalants.net

Information on the dangers, history, effects, signs, use, and abuse of inhalants is provided at this Web site. Products used include solvents, aerosols, gases, and nitrates, which are all very dangerous to your health. Read more about inhalant abuse.

▶NAADAC, The Association for Addiction Professionals

NAADAC focuses on drug, tobacco, alcohol, and gaming addictions in an effort to create healthier families and communities through prevention, intervention, and quality treatment. The organization supports research, policies, and funding for the prevention, understanding, and treatment of addictions.

▶Narcotics Anonymous

Based on the Twelve Step Program, Narcotics Anonymous can be found in over one hundred countries. You can follow the links to find worldwide contact and meeting information. Bulletins, reports, and periodicals are also available for the reader.

▶NIDA InfoFacts: Inhalants

You will learn about the health hazards of using inhalants, including the risk of Sudden Sniffing Death Syndrome, which can result from a single use of inhalants. An overview of inhalants is also provided as well as a list of the most common ones.

Report Links

The Internet sites described below can be accessed at http://www.myreportlinks.com

▶**Partnership for a Drug-Free America**

The Partnership for a Drug-Free America focuses its efforts on reducing substance abuse in America. You will find a recent study on teen drug use, an e-newsletter you can sign up for, and stories about real people.

▶**Rising to the Challenges of Inhalant Abuse**

The World Health Organization estimates that tens of millions of children are abusing inhalants, especially kids who live on the streets. Inhalants are cheap and accessible to children. Learn more about what is being done to overcome the problem of inhalant addiction.

▶**The Story of a Teen Girl's Huffing Addiction**

Megan Hakeman's story of her addiction to household inhalants is informative. Read the important lessons she learned in treatment and why she is now sober and happy. To read Megan's mother's story, click on the link at the bottom of the page.

▶**Street Terms: Drugs and the Drug Trade, Drug Type: Inhalants**

Learn the terms that are used to describe inhalants and the activities surrounding their use. A valuable resource for parents, teachers, and students.

▶**StreetDrugs.org: Inhalants**

Easy accessibility and low cost make inhalants popular among kids. An overview of inhalants is presented along with information on user statistics, effects, and signs of abuse.

▶**Teen Success: Inhalants**

Many teenagers do not realize that sniffing or huffing inhalants can kill them. They believe it is a cheap and easy high with no long-term effects. Learn the truth about inhalants at this Web site.

▶**What You Need to Know About Drugs: Inhalants**

This fact sheet explains what inhalants are and what they are sometimes called. It also provides information on how inhalants are used and how they affect the body.

▶**What's Up with Inhalants?**

Common household products found in most homes are abused as inhalants. You will find information on how they are used, their nicknames, and the mental and physical dangers inhalants can cause.

INHALANT FACTS

✗ More than 18 million Americans have abused inhalants.

✗ More than a million Americans each year try inhalants for the first time.

✗ Approximately one hundred American adolescents die each year from ingesting inhalants.

✗ About half of those who die from inhalant abuse are victims of Sudden Sniffing Death Syndrome.

✗ Each year, hundreds of Americans suffer serious, permanent damage to their vital organs due to inhalant abuse.

✗ Based on a 2003 survey, 11.2 percent of twelfth graders and 15.8 percent of eighth graders admitted using an inhalant in their lifetime.

✗ According to the same survey, 1.5 percent of high school seniors and 4.1 percent of eighth graders admitted abusing inhalants in the past month.

✗ In 2003, only 40.3 percent of eighth graders said they felt that using inhalants once or twice was a "great risk."

✗ Also in 2003, 85.1 percent of eighth graders and 89.8 percent of tenth graders disapproved of people who tried inhalants once or twice.

✗ About 50 percent of sniffers and huffers abuse inhalants with friends.

✗ About 80 percent of inhalant abusers have friends or close acquaintances who also abuse inhalants.

✗ More than one thousand products are classified as inhalants.

✗ Thirty-eight states have adopted laws preventing the sale, use, and/or distribution to minors of products commonly abused as inhalants.

Fast Drying
SPRAY ENAMEL
• Interior
• Exterior

FE-505 RED

Chapter 1

THE SILENT EPIDEMIC

Each month, more than four hundred thousand American adolescents sniff inhalants.[1] They inhale the fumes of paint, markers, glue, nail polish, gasoline, and a thousand other toxic products. It is often called sniffing or "huffing" (inhaling rigorously through the mouth).

Many kids believe sniffing and huffing is harmless fun. They are deathly wrong. Just ask the parents of Johnson Bryant.* Their son was a varsity athlete as well as an excellent student. He enjoyed a warm relationship with his mother and father. Johnson died after huffing a gas called butane.

"It's frightening to see your son in a body bag," grieved his mother. "When the coroner said it looked like he'd inhaled butane, I thought, This is something I see on *20/20*. . . . There is no pain like losing a child. . . . I talk to Johnson sometimes. Sometimes I yell at him. Sometimes I say, 'I miss you, baby.'"[2]

▶ Sniffing, Huffing, and Dying

Each year, approximately one hundred children and teens die from abusing inhalants. Hundreds more suffer serious, permanent damage to their lungs, heart, and other vital organs. Millions of kids do not understand how dangerous it is to inhale toxic chemicals. According to Harvey Weiss, director of the National Inhalant Prevention Coalition, inhaling gasoline vapors is no different than drinking the poisonous fuel.[3]

From the early 1990s to the early 2000s, the number of young people who abused inhalants nearly doubled. About 20

*While the stories of abuse in this book are real, many of the names have been changed.

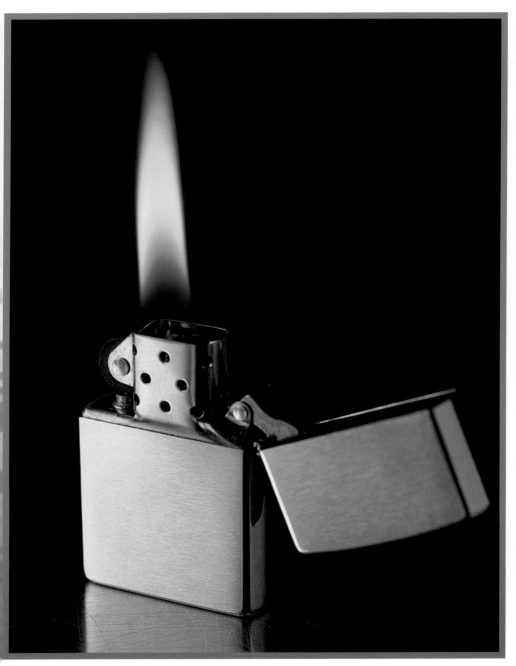

▲ *Butane is a gas that is used to fuel lighters such as this one, as well as lighters that are used to light barbecue grills. Inhaling butane can be deadly.*

percent of eighth graders—kids just thirteen or fourteen years old—admitted trying inhalants. Inhalant abuse has been labeled the "silent epidemic."

"Inhalants are the fourth most abused substances in the United States among students from grades eight through twelve," said Dr. Patricia Block. "Alcohol, cigarettes, and marijuana are the top three. Inhalants are higher on the list than crack cocaine. Inhalants are readily available, cheap to purchase, and hard to control."[4]

Those who breathe in inhalants may achieve a brief high. They might also experience headaches and dizziness, and become violently ill. With repeated use, inhalants could damage their lungs, kidneys, and liver. Users could go deaf or blind. Those who

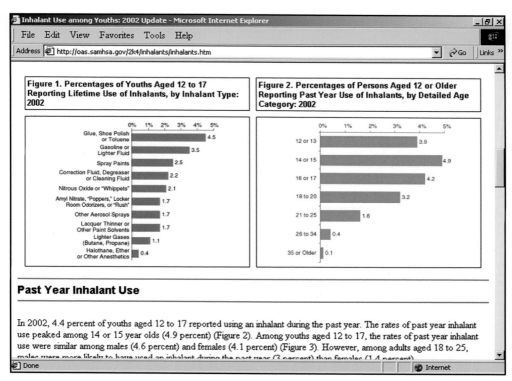

According to these graphs, fourteen or fifteen year olds are the most likely to use inhalants, and the most common forms of inhalants used are glue, shoe polish, or Toluene.

sniff and huff destroy many of their brain cells, which could seriously diminish their ability to learn, remember, and solve problems. Some users experience Sudden Sniffing Death Syndrome (SSDS), dying from just one sniff of a toxic chemical.

"It's a very deadly practice," said Weiss. "Any time you use an inhalant, it could kill you—the first time or the fiftieth time."[5]

Tragic Tales

At age sixteen, Trevor began to inhale the fumes of hair spray and air freshener. "One night after partying, I ended up in the hospital scared and unable to breathe," he said. Trevor survived, but the toxic chemicals had permanently damaged his body. "At times I have led a fairly normal life," he wrote a decade later. "At other times I have been totally bedridden, using oxygen and nebulizers and inhalers, etc. etc., to make it through. I have often gone to bed at night wondering if I would wake to see the next day."[6]

Trevor listed his symptoms as "dizziness, lightheadedness, weakness, fatigue, hot flashes, shortness of breath, loss of balance, rapid heartbeat, loss of appetite, nausea, vomiting, weight loss, muscle tremors, ringing, and pressure in ears."

Trevor adores his beautiful, young daughter. But "due to my health problems, I am unable to run and play and do the things that my daughter wants to do," he wrote.[7]

Robert began huffing at age nine. He experienced his first high the first time he tried it. But, because of tolerance to the chemicals, he never achieved such euphoria again, though he kept trying and trying. "It doesn't work," he wrote. "It's like getting caught in a whirlpool. The harder you fight, the more you go down."[8]

Robert spent time in three rehabilitation programs, one halfway house, and was in therapy for years. Yet no one could reverse the damage that inhalants had done to his body. "I have twitches that won't go away," he wrote. "I get nosebleeds, my sense of smell comes and goes, [and] my memory is worse than

COMMONLY ABUSED COMMERCIAL PRODUCTS	
Adhesives	Model airplane glue, rubber cement, household glue
Aerosols	Spray paint, hair spray, air freshener, deodorant, fabric protector
Anesthetics	Nitrous oxide, ether, chloroform
Cleaning Agents	Dry cleaning fluid, spot remover, degreaser
Food products	Vegetable cooking spray, whippets (nitrous oxide)
Gases	Nitrous oxide, butane, propane, helium
Solvents and Gases	Nail polish remover, paint thinner, typing correction fluid and thinner, toxic markers, pure toluene, toluol, cigar lighter fluid, gasoline

Source: National Inhalant Prevention Coalition

my eighty-four-year-old grandfather's." He added, tragically, that "I lost the respect of my family and friends."[9]

Trevor and Robert at least are alive to tell their stories. Seth was not so lucky. Seth wanted desperately to end his addiction to inhalants. "He told me, 'Mom, I so much want to live,'" recalled his mother. "'I don't want to get high, but I just can't stop.'"[10] In September 1999, Seth moved to San Diego to enroll in college. He died two days later with a plastic bag on his head and a can of shaving gel at his side.

HISTORY OF INHALANTS

People got high on fumes long before aerosol cans were invented. In ancient Greece, a woman traditionally would enter a small chamber in the mountains. Inside, she would inhale ethylene gas that rose through a crack in the ground. While high from the fumes, she would utter spiritual observations.

Over the centuries, people in many cultures inhaled vapors. They burned spices and leaves and inhaled the smoke. For them, it was part of religious worship. Centuries later, millions of people would sniff inhalants, but only to get a cheap high.

▶ No Laughing Matter

In the mid-1800s, some Americans began to abuse a new painkiller called nitrous oxide or "laughing gas." In 1844, Gardner Quincy Colton, a medical student

Nitrous oxide or "laughing gas" is commonly used by doctors and dentists to numb pain. It is also used to boost performance in some automobiles. However, people also purchase nitrous oxide tanks such as these to inhale the drugs. Inhaling too much can kill a person.

in Connecticut, staged a nitrous oxide exhibition. His ad for the event stated: "Forty gallons of gas will be prepared and administered to all in the audience who desire to inhale it . . . . The effect of the Gas is to make those who inhale it either Laugh, Sing, Dance, Speak or Fight, and so forth, according to the leading trait of their character."[1]

Colton thought that inhaling nitrous oxide would be as harmless for adults as having a couple alcoholic drinks. He did not realize the side effects of nitrous oxide, which included death. A hundred fifty years later, nitrous oxide would become a widely abused inhalant.

In the 1800s, those seeking a high inhaled the vapors of two other anesthetics: ether and chloroform. Some people got high on gas during parties called "ether frolics." A century later, other toxic chemicals were created and abused. In the early 1900s, companies manufactured products from petroleum. These products included solvents, thinners, and glue, all of which would be used to get high.

In the 1950s, some Americans inhaled the fumes of gasoline. They often experienced hallucinations and broke into bizarre tantrums. Glue sniffing became a trend in the United States in the early 1960s. By 1965, glue sniffing occurred in every state of the union. By 1968, thirteen states had passed anti-glue-sniffing legislation.

Glue was not the only abused inhalant in the 1960s. Some young people sniffed the vapors of nail polish remover and aerosol cans, such as hair spray. Aerosols contain highly toxic fluorocarbons, that have killed numerous abusers. Inhalant abuse diminished somewhat in the 1970s, but by the 1980s, it was on the rise again. In a 1983 survey, 14 percent of high school seniors admitted using inhalants at some point during their lives.[2]

▶ A Modern Problem

While law enforcement focused on crack cocaine in the 1980s, thousands of adolescents were quietly abusing inhalants. For the price of an after-school snack, teenagers could buy their drug of choice at the local department store. Younger kids found their inhalants in their parents' closets, as well as their classroom. They sniffed the fumes of glue, paint, felt-tipped pens, aerosols, typewriter correction fluid, and other easily obtainable products.

In the 1990s, inhalant abuse skyrocketed. By 1997, 20 percent of American eighth graders admitted to using inhalants.

△ *This homeless young man is sniffing glue on a street in El Salvador. Glue sniffing has become a worldwide problem. Some young people sniff glue to temporarily forget their problems, but do not realize that it can lead to permanent brain damage.*

By 1999, approximately 17 million Americans had sniffed some type of fumes to get high at least once in their lifetime. In 1999 alone, more than one hundred thousand Americans sought treatment for inhalant use.

By this time, kids had developed a method for abusing inhalants. In a practice called bagging, some tied plastic bags around their heads and filled them with the gas of aerosol cans. Others soaked rags in chemicals and inhaled the fumes through their mouths, which they called huffing. At raves (all-night dance parties) and concerts, vendors sold balloons filled with nitrous oxide. Users sucked the gas for a cheap high. Also at these venues, dealers peddled "poppers" (amyl or butyl nitrite). Sniffing this

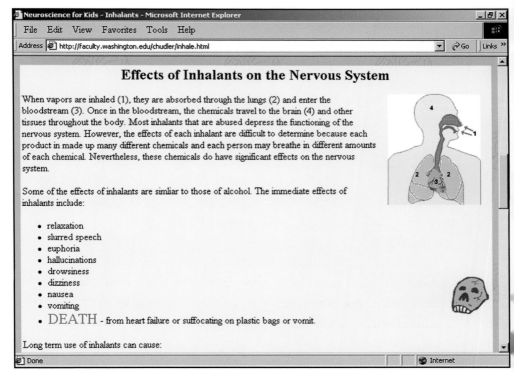

When a user inhales vapors, the chemicals are absorbed through the lungs, enter into the bloodstream, and then travel to the brain. These chemicals act as depressants on the nervous system, causing slurred speech, hallucinations, dizziness, and more.

dangerous liquid gave users a quick "rush." Many of them were soon rushed to the emergency room.

From 1994 to 2001, more than seven hundred American teenagers died from using inhalants. Moreover, the age that young people started to abuse inhalants became younger and younger. For example, in 1997, 13 percent of eighth graders reported using inhalants within the past month.[3] "Among twelve-year-olds," said Cindi Bookout of the Alliance for Consumer Education in 2001, "inhalants are the most frequently used illicit substance."[4]

Getting the Message Out

By 2000, thirty-eight states had adopted laws preventing the sale, use, and/or distribution to minors of products commonly abused as inhalants. Such laws had little effect, however. Kids still could find paint thinner in the garage, a whipped cream can in the fridge, or a nitrous oxide balloon at a party. From 2000 to 2002, the number of emergency department mentions of inhalants rose from 1,141 to 1,496.[5]

Despite the frightening statistics, millions of adolescents viewed inhalants as fairly harmless. According to a study in 2002, only 43 percent of eighth graders believed that trying inhalants was dangerous.[6] In the new millennium, many organizations, schools, and parents have been trying to educate students about the dangers of inhalants.

Diane Stem, whose son, Ricky, died from inhalant abuse, became a tireless crusader against inhalants. She wrote: "Since Ricky's death, year after year, we . . . continue reading the tragic headlines with stories, many times identical to ours. Parents left dealing with the loss of a child to a killer they had never even heard of. . . . We hope to spare another family, maybe your family, from this nightmare."[7]

EFFECTS OF INHALANTS

Life seemed to be pretty easy for Anthony. He was an A student, a good athlete, and a popular kid. He did have one bad habit: sniffing the fumes of air freshener. Shortly before his fourteenth birthday, Anthony died of a heart attack.

With each sniff of an inhalant, a person damages his or her body. One sniff could prove fatal. "It's like playing Russian roulette," said Dr. H. Westley Clark, director of the federal Center for Substance Abuse Treatment.[1]

According to the National Institute on Drug Abuse, "Inhalants are substances whose vapors can be inhaled to produce a mind-altering effect."[2] These chemicals are not only harmful, but they are also readily available. Young people have abused more than a thousand products designated as inhalants.

▶ Four Ways to Inhale

Inhalant abusers have found four different ways to get high: sniffing, huffing, ballooning, and bagging. Sniffers breathe in fumes through their noses, while huffers inhale fumes rigorously through their mouths. Serious huffers will soak a rag with their favorite chemical and inhale from that. Through ballooning, abusers inhale gas (most commonly nitrous oxide) from a balloon. Bagging is the most extreme form of inhalant abuse. Users actually seal a plastic bag around their head and fill it with toxic gas. Many such abusers have died with the bag still on their head.

You should not inhale or consume any product that is not clearly a food or drink. To be sure, read the label. Do not ingest or breathe in products labeled "poison," "toxic," "danger,"

These helium-filled balloons appear to be a harmless party favor. However, some people sell balloons filled with toxic chemicals that people use to get high. Inhaling chemicals in this way is known as ballooning.

"warning," "flammable," "corrosive," or "do not ingest." If you have any doubts at all about a product, ask an adult for advice.

Solvents, Gases, and Nitrites

Scientists classify inhalants into three categories: solvents, gases, and nitrites. All three forms are toxic.

Solvents are liquids that give off toxic vapors. Solvents are depressants, meaning they slow down the activity of the body's central nervous system. The National Institute on Drug Abuse breaks down solvents into two groups. Its doctors call the first group "industrial or household solvents or solvent-containing products." These include gasoline, glue, paint thinners, paint removers, degreasers, and dry-cleaning fluids. The second group is "art or office supply solvents." Examples include correction fluids, felt-tip marker fluid, and electronic contact cleaners.

When discussing inhalants, scientists separate gases into three groups. One category is household and commercial products, including butane lighters, propane tanks, whipped cream aerosol cans, and refrigerant gases. A second group includes household aerosol propellants. These are gases that you spray, such as spray paints, hair spray, deodorant spray, and fabric protector spray. The third category is medical anesthetic gases: ether, chloroform, halothane, and nitrous oxide. Like solvents, gases are also classified as depressants.

Nitrites are chemicals made from nitrogen and oxygen. When inhaled, nitrites dilate blood vessels and relax muscles. Aliphatic nitrites are found in room odorizers. Amyl nitrite, a prescribed heart medicine, is often abused as a party drug. Butyl nitrite, once used in perfumes and antifreeze, is now an illegal substance but still widely abused.

Inhalants' Short-Term Effects

When a person sniffs or huffs an inhalant, the toxic fumes go straight to hsi or her lungs and then get absorbed into the

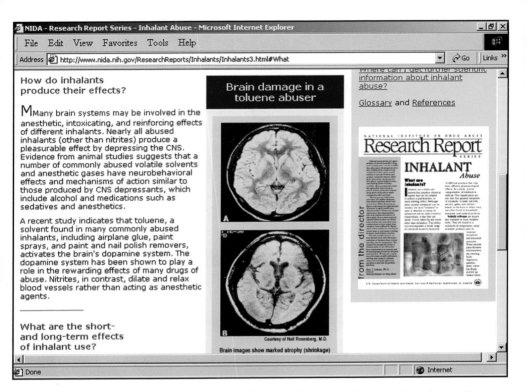

NIDA - Research Report Series - Inhalant Abuse - Microsoft Internet Explorer

File   Edit   View   Favorites   Tools   Help

Address 📄 http://www.nida.nih.gov/ResearchReports/Inhalants/Inhalants3.html#What   ▾ 🔗Go   Links »

How do inhalants produce their effects?

Many brain systems may be involved in the anesthetic, intoxicating, and reinforcing effects of different inhalants. Nearly all abused inhalants (other than nitrites) produce a pleasurable effect by depressing the CNS. Evidence from animal studies suggests that a number of commonly abused volatile solvents and anesthetic gases have neurobehavioral effects and mechanisms of action similar to those produced by CNS depressants, which include alcohol and medications such as sedatives and anesthetics.

A recent study indicates that toluene, a solvent found in many commonly abused inhalants, including airplane glue, paint sprays, and paint and nail polish removers, activates the brain's dopamine system. The dopamine system has been shown to play a role in the rewarding effects of many drugs of abuse. Nitrites, in contrast, dilate and relax blood vessels rather than acting as anesthetic agents.

What are the short- and long-term effects of inhalant use?

Brain damage in a toluene abuser

Where can I get further scientific information about inhalant abuse?

Glossary and References

Research Report SERIES

INHALANT Abuse

Courtesy of Neil Rosenberg, M.D.

Brain images show marked atrophy (shrinkage)

Done   🖳 Internet

△ *These images show the difference between the brains of an inhalant abuser (B) and a non-abuser (A). The abuser's brain has not only shrunk, but it also has empty spaces within it.*

bloodstream. From there, the toxic chemicals head are observed into the muscles and major organs, including the heart and brain. "It gets pumped straight up there," said Harvey Weiss, director of the National Inhalant Prevention Coalition. "It goes over the blood-brain barrier and eats away at your brain cells."[3]

Because the chemicals go directly to the brain, the user feels their effects within seconds. Inhalant highs can last from several minutes to an hour. At first, the user experiences a mild euphoria. He becomes light-headed, excited, and numb. The inhalants then reach the central nervous system, which includes the brain and spinal cord. Inhalants that are depressants (solvents and gases) depress the central nervous system. Thus, the person becomes less inhibited. He may become dizzy, sleepy, and giddy. His hands and feet might tingle or go numb. He might slur his speech or have trouble walking. He could get a headache, nausea, chest or stomach pains, double vision, or ringing in the ears.

If a user inhales a large amount of toxic chemicals, she could experience more severe effects. She could feel dazed and confused or have trouble breathing. She might experience hallucinations (imaginary sights and sounds) and vomit repeatedly. She could pass out, fall into a coma, or even die.

▶ The Dangers of Continued Use

After the inhalant high is over, most of the toxic chemicals leave the body. They are eliminated through the lungs, kidneys, and skin. However, some of the chemicals stay in the body forever. They are stored in the fatty tissue of the muscles, brain, and other major organs. You can imagine, therefore, how dangerous it is to abuse inhalants multiple times. The more people abuse inhalants, the more poison they are storing in their bodies. This can damage the liver and kidneys, hinder breathing, and cause some types of cancer.

Moreover, with each repeated use, the body develops tolerance. This means the user will need a stronger dose of an inhalant to achieve the initial high. A person who took five sniffs of an inhalant the first time may need ten sniffs the next time to reach the same state. With this pattern of behavior, the amount of toxic chemicals stored in the body increases greatly.

Some people who use inhalants become physically and mentally addicted to them. They enjoy the high and want to attain it again and again. They become preoccupied with the drug, which usually means that the rest of their life suffers. Routine abusers tend to lose interest in friends and family, school, and hobbies. When off the drug, they suffer from withdrawal symptoms, such as chills, headaches, cramps, and tremors.

DAMAGE TO BODY CAUSED BY INHALANTS	
Acoustic Nerve and Muscle	Destruction of cells that relay sound to the brain may cause deafness.
Blood	The oxygen-carrying capacity of the blood can be inhibited.
Bone Marrow	Components containing benzene have been shown to cause leukemia.
Brain	Damage is caused to the cerebral cortex and the cerebellum, resulting in personality changes, memory impairment, hallucinations, loss of coordination, and slurred speech.
Heart	Sudden Sniffing Death Syndrome (SSDS), an unexpected disturbance in the heart's rhythm, may cause fatal cardiac arrhythmias (heart failure).
Kidneys	The kidneys' ability to control the amount of acid in the blood may be impaired. Kidney stones may develop after use is terminated.
Liver	Gathering of fatty tissue may cause liver damage.
Lungs	Damaged lungs and impaired breathing occur with repeated use.
Muscle	Chronic use can lead to muscle wasting and reduced muscle tone and strength.
Peripheral Nervous System	Damage to the nerves may result in numbness, tingling, and paralysis.
Skin	A severe rash around the nose and mouth, referred to as "glue sniffer's rash," may result.

Source: National Inhalant Prevention Coalition

"Once a young person becomes addicted to inhalants, it is very difficult to get them off," said Dr. Patricia Block. "It is all but impossible without professional help. All the while, the inhalants are ruining their bodies."[4]

A young woman named Star was part of a group of inhalant abusers in Australia. She talked about her friends, those addicted to toxic chemicals. "One month they're doing fine and next month they're back on [inhalants] and the next month they've passed away," she said. "Just all leads down hill, to be quite honest."[5]

The symptoms of inhalants differ depending on the product. However, all inhalants damage the brain, and it does not take a brain surgeon to understand why. "When you put paint remover on paint, it just eats it away," said Harvey Weiss. "When you sniff it, it starts to eat away your brain."[6]

Inhalants kill brain cells. They can lead to headaches and memory loss and harm one's problem-solving ability. Some forget how to do simple math equations. "When I'm talking," said one inhalant abuser who had suffered brain damage, "I'll forget what I just said two seconds ago."[7] Tragically, many abusers have to resign themselves to menial work for the rest of their lives.

Certain inhalants, such as glue and aerosols, can cause chronic coughing, nausea, dizziness, and stomach pain. They can damage one's vision and hearing. Abusers may develop rashes around their nose or mouth and have nosebleeds. They could become chronically tired, lose too much weight, or experience muscle weakness or limb spasms. Some abusers lose control over their bowel movements or ability to urinate. Others lose control over their behavior. They become aggressive and violent, posing a risk to themselves and others.

Inhalants can damage major organs besides the brain, including the kidneys, liver, and heart. They have also been linked to impotence in men. Some abusers suffer from hepatitis—inflammation of the liver. Aerosols are especially hard on the heart. They cause irregular heartbeats and heart failure. Those who inhale rubber cement stand a greater chance of getting leukemia. Gasoline sniffing can result in lead poisoning, which can cause dementia and muscle paralysis. Abuse of amyl and butyl nitrites has been linked to a sometimes fatal cancer called Kaposi's sarcoma that causes painful sores on and inside the body. If a woman abuses inhalants while pregnant, she could seriously harm or even kill her baby.

Inhalant abuse also can cause Sudden Sniffing Death Syndrome (SSDS). In such instances, inhalation of a toxic chemical stops the heart. Of the five hundred-plus Americans who died from inhalant abuse from 1996 through 1999, 55 percent died

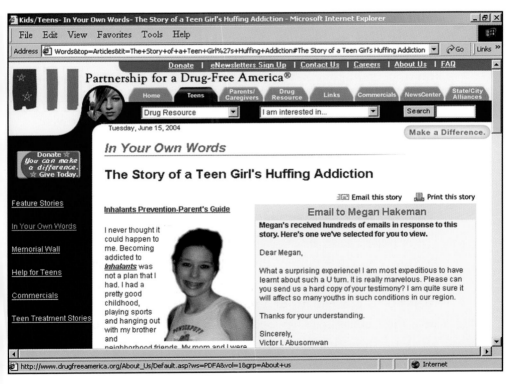

▲ Megan Hakeman began huffing at the age of thirteen. Within a year she was addicted to inhalants and, thanks to her loving family, in treatment. Fortunately, Megan's story is a successful one. By her fifteenth birthday, Megan was clean and sober.

Huffing or sniffing gasoline can cause lead poisoning, which can cause paralysis and dementia.

from SSDS. Chillingly, SSDS can strike any inhalant abuser, even first-timers. Children have dropped dead just from sniffing glue.

Inhalants can kill in other ways, too. Some suffer from asphyxia. In such cases, toxic gases limit oxygen in the air going into the lungs. Breathing then stops. Other users choke to death on their own vomit. Many "baggers" suffocate to death, as they cut off oxygen to their lungs. Other inhalant abusers have died by acting carelessly while high.

In 1999, five teenage girls from Pennsylvania died after their car spun out of control and crashed. The medical examiner stated that "intoxication in the driver developed to the point that she could no longer control the car."[8] The driver had not been drinking or smoking marijuana. She was not high on cocaine or ecstasy. She had been sniffing from a bottle of computer cleaner.

Chapter 4 ▶

INHALANT ABUSE

No sensible person would put poison into his or her body. Yet more than 18 million Americans have abused inhalants, which are toxic chemicals. Most abusers are very young, including children in the early years of grade school.

The high from inhalants is not considered as great as those of other drugs, so why do so many young people abuse them?

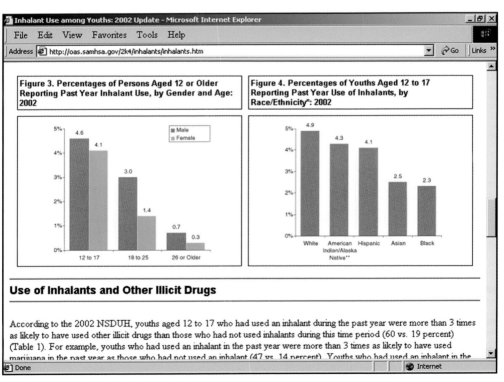

▲ According to the National Survey on Drug Use and Health, inhalants are most frequently used by white males between the ages of twelve and seventeen.

Harvey Weiss summed it up. "Kids can get it at home, at school, almost anyplace," he said. "A child does not have to go to a pusher to get the stuff." Moreover, he added, "kids are generally uninformed about the dangers, and parents and educators don't talk about them."[1]

Who Abuses Inhalants—And Why?

According to Weiss, inhalant abuse cuts across all racial and social boundaries.[2] It cannot be dismissed as a "male thing" or an "inner-city problem." The only significant trait of inhalant users is that they are, on average, the youngest of all drug abusers. Surveys show that the most likely abusers of inhalants are kids from ages seven to seventeen.

Why does inhalant abuse mostly occur with young people? First of all, older drug abusers usually opt for drugs that produce "stronger and longer lasting" highs. They prefer such drugs as marijuana, ecstasy, or crack cocaine (all of which are illegal and harmful). The older users often can afford such drugs, and they know how to hook up with drug dealers. The easiest way for most adolescents to get high is to grab a glue bottle from their desk or nail polish from the closet.

Kids abuse inhalants for reasons other than accessibility. For one thing, inhalant abuse can be easy to hide. Sniffers can keep markers, glue, or type-correction fluid in their pants pocket. Unlike cigarettes, marijuana, and crack, inhalants do not create a cloud of smoke that fills up the bedroom or restroom. Also, inhalants appeal to kids because they produce a quick high. As with candy bars and video games, inhalants can lead to instant pleasure. Fumes go straight to the brain, triggering a high within seconds. Unlike candy bars and video games, inhalant abuse can be very harmful.

There is an old saying, "idle hands are the devil's tools." This means that when people are bored they tend to get into trouble. Many inhalant abusers can attest to this. One junior high student remembered the night he wanted to get high. He invited his friends over, hoping they would bring marijuana, but they did not. After they left, "I got so bored I tried falling asleep and couldn't," he wrote. "So I thought of huffing." The boy soaked a sock with chemicals and huffed the vapors. "I woke up in the middle of the night and had SEVERE stomach pains," he wrote. "I actually prayed for me to die."[3]

A myth about inhalants is that kids abuse them alone. According to a study reported in the *American Journal of Drug and Alcohol Abuse*, 52 percent of sniffers and huffers abused inhalants with friends. Actually, the desire to fit in with a certain

STREET TERMS FOR INHALANTS	
Air blast	Laughing Gas (nitrous oxide)
Ames (amyl nitrite)	Medusa
Amys (amyl nitrite)	Moon gas
Bagging (using inhalants)	Oz
Bolt (isobutyl nitrite)	Pearls (amyl nitrite)
Boppers (amyl nitrite)	Poor man's pot
Buzz Bomb (nitrous oxide)	Poppers (isobutyl nitrite)
Climax (isobutyl nitrite)	Quicksilver (isobutyl nitrite)
Discorama	Rush (isobutyl nitrite)
Glading (using inhalants)	Shoot the breeze (use nitrous oxide)
Gluey (one who sniffs or inhales glue)	Snappers (isobutyl nitrite)
Hardware (isobutyl nitrite)	Snorting (using inhalants)
Hippie crack	Thrust (isobutyl nitrite)
Huff	Toncho (octane booster)
Huffing (breathing in an inhalant)	Whippets (nitrous oxide)
Kick	Whiteout (isobutyl nitrite)

Source: National Inhalant Prevention Coalition

group is a big reason why kids start using inhalants. The same study reported that 81 percent of inhalant abusers had friends or close acquaintances who also ingested inhalants.[4]

Poor family relationships are also linked to inhalant abuse. Studies show that young people who do not interact much with their parents are much more likely to try inhalants. Some young people rebel against their parents by abusing inhalants. Inevitably, they end up hurting their family members and themselves.

▷ No Reason Is a Good Reason

No one on planet Earth—no physician, chemist, or psychiatrist— has found a good reason to inhale chemicals for pleasure. Medically speaking, no one needs an artificial high. People need things like food, water, sunshine, fresh air, and exercise. But getting high on drugs is not a physical drive that your body requires. Many first-time inhalant users, in fact, do not even like the effect. Many simply report feeling "weird," "light-headed," or "naseous." Many people would find more pleasure licking an ice cream cone than inhaling chemicals.

Of course, the harmful effects of abusing inhalants are downright frightening. The more huffing a person does, the more damage he or she does to the body. Boredom, of course, is not an excuse to sniff or huff. Those with too much time on their hands should pursue worthwhile or at least harmless activities, not destructive ones.

Many kids sniff and huff simply because their friends are into it. Yet peer pressure is certainly no reason to inhale chemicals. If your friend is enthusiastic about inhalants, he likely does not know how harmful they are. Nevertheless, he may pressure you into trying them, putting you in an awkward position. You may not know how to respond. In the heat of the moment, you might find it easier to say "OK" than to think of a good reason to say no. Here are some effective ways to refuse inhalants:

• Give solid reasons, such as "Did you read the label? You are inhaling poison into your brain," or "No way! I just read about a kid who died from sniffing glue."

• Suggest alternatives: "Forget that; we should go to a movie."

• Do not get sucked into a discussion or argument. Just give them an emphatic "no."

• If talking does not work, just say good-bye and leave. Odds are, in a few days your friend will not remember or care about what had happened. If he or she does not shrug off the argument, or if that person feels that he or she can only be friends with people that inhale with him or her, then it probably is time to let the friendship fizzle.

▷ Small Sniffs Lead to Big Trouble

Perhaps a few kids in your school think it is okay or even cool to abuse inhalants. These kids are a small minority. Almost everyone disapproves of inhalants, including grade-school kids, high school students, and parents. Moreover, schools and law enforcement officials do not tolerate inhalant abuse.

According to a report by the Office of National Drug Control Policy, 90 percent of eighth graders and 92 percent of tenth graders did not approve of regular inhalant use.[5] In short, sniffing and huffing are definitely not cool.

Most inhalant abusers do not realize the trouble they can get into. Chronic huffers get so sick and/or reek of chemicals that their parents inevitably discover their secret.

Spray guns are a household tool that help people ▷ *paint large areas quickly. However, they can also be used as a powerful and extremely harmful way to inhale paint fumes.*

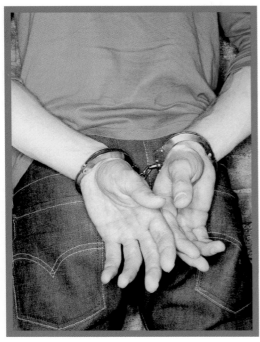

Although many inhalants are household products that can be obtained easily, that does not mean that they cannot get a user in trouble. In many states it is illegal to inhale chemicals for the purpose of getting high.

Schools take inhalant abuse very seriously. Many school districts include inhalants in their drug policies. Students who use and/or deal inhalants can be suspended or even expelled. Often, the reason for the suspension spreads throughout the school, adding to the user's shame.

More and more, lawmakers are creating and stiffening laws related to inhalants. Most states regulate the sale of inhalants to minors. Massachusetts, for example, requires retailers to "card" people who buy glue or rubber cement. Those who sell inhalants to minors, be it store owners or drug dealers, can be arrested and jailed. In many states, getting high on inhalants is against the law. Sniffers and huffers can be subjected to mandatory drug treatment, fined, or even sent to jail. No matter how you look at it, abusing inhalants leads to nothing but trouble.

AVOIDING INHALANTS

Writing in a teen magazine, a young woman discussed the loss of her thirteen-year-old brother to inhalant abuse. "He died in my arms at the county hospital," she wrote. "I was the one who took him to the hospital after some of his friends had a 'sniffing party.' He sniffed his way to his own death. He didn't know that inhalants could kill him."[1]

Thousands of young people have suffered severe health problems or died because they were not paying attention to inhalants' harmful effects. Millions of Americans—children, parents, even many teachers—need to learn about the dangers of huffing and sniffing. In previous chapters, you learned why you should avoid inhalants. This chapter explains how to help inhalant abusers and how to educate others about their dangers.

▶ Warning Signs

If a person is abusing inhalants, it is critical that he or she stops immediately. Tragically, many users continue to damage their bodies because no one notices that they have a problem. A person may indeed be an inhalant abuser if he or she exhibits any of these warning signs:

Inhaling spray paint and products from other types of ▶ aerosol cans is a common form of abuse. One way to tell if a person may be abusing inhalants is if you see them with paint stains on his or her face or clothes.

- Breath or clothes smell like chemicals

- Possesses inhalant paraphernalia, including inhalant products (such as aerosol cans), rags that smell like chemicals, or stained plastic bags

- Sores or rashes around the nose or mouth

- Paint marks around the nose or mouth

- Red, watery eyes

- Loss of appetite

- Nosebleeds, nose drips, or sneezing

- Coughing or breathing trouble

- Loss of coordination

- Intoxicated behavior

- Slurs words or speech does not make sense

- Disorientation, confusion, memory loss, or slow responses to questions

- Irritability, moodiness, violent behavior

- Neglects personal appearance

- Becomes withdrawn and apathetic

- Loses interest in school, work and/or, sports

If a person in your presence is having an adverse reaction to an inhalant, you must take action. Immediately ventilate the area; take the chemicals away from the user and open the windows. Just as quickly, shout for an adult to help you and/or call 911. All the while remain calm—the user does not need additional stress.

▷ Where to Go for Help

If you have a problem with inhalants, you need to seek help immediately. It is virtually impossible, according to experts, to beat inhalant addiction on your own. "It's psychologically addictive," said Harvey Weiss, director of the National Inhalant

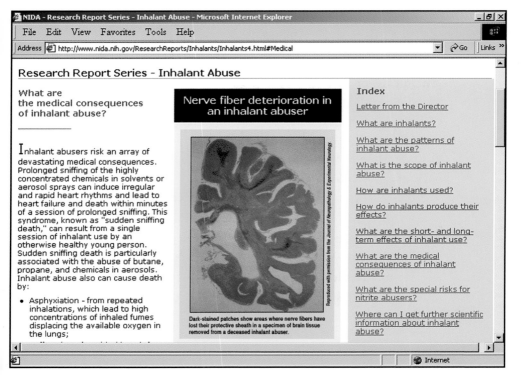

Research Report Series - Inhalant Abuse

What are the medical consequences of inhalant abuse?

Nerve fiber deterioration in an inhalant abuser

Inhalant abusers risk an array of devastating medical consequences. Prolonged sniffing of the highly concentrated chemicals in solvents or aerosol sprays can induce irregular and rapid heart rhythms and lead to heart failure and death within minutes of a session of prolonged sniffing. This syndrome, known as "sudden sniffing death," can result from a single session of inhalant use by an otherwise healthy young person. Sudden sniffing death is particularly associated with the abuse of butane, propane, and chemicals in aerosols. Inhalant abuse also can cause death by:

- Asphyxiation - from repeated inhalations, which lead to high concentrations of inhaled fumes displacing the available oxygen in the lungs;

Dark-stained patches show areas where nerve fibers have lost their protective sheath in a specimen of brain tissue removed from a deceased inhalant abuser.

Internet

△ Brain damage, as shown by the dark spots on this image of brain tissue taken of a deceased inhalant abuser, is the one of the most significant effects of inhalant abuse.

Prevention Coalition. "It's a tough habit to kick—harder than cocaine," in his opinion.[2]

If your friend or loved one is hooked on inhalants, you need to take action. Thinking that "it's probably no big deal, he'll be all right" is the wrong decision. You probably should not approach him directly about the problem. He likely will be defensive and could become violent, especially if he is high.

If you or someone you know has an inhalant problem, it is best to contact an adult you can trust. The adult could be a parent, relative, teacher, school nurse, or doctor. Often it is smart to talk to your school counselor, who likely is trained to handle such matters. If you are an inhalant user but are too nervous to discuss the problem with someone you know, help is available for you, too. You just need to take the first step.

A good place to start is the National Inhalant Prevention Coalition. Also, the NAADAC boasts the nation's largest network of alcoholism and drug-abuse treatment professionals. Other helpful organizations include the National Drug & Alcohol Treatment Hotline, National Helplines, and Narcotics Anonymous. (Look for the phone numbers of these organizations in the back of this book.)

Those seeking help with addiction should also check for listings in their phone book. It might list a local drug treatment center, walk-in medical clinic, or crisis center. You or an adult may need to contact your local Poison Control Center. They can explain to you the toxicology of the product that has been abused and perhaps give you a medical referral. You can also call your local library or hospital for advice.

▷ Treatment for Inhalant Abuse

Inhalants can harm a person in so many ways. They can cause physical ailments; brain damage; and behavioral, emotional, and social problems. Thus, treatment for inhalant abuse can be quite long and involved.

Medical staff members will first interview and assess the patient. They will ask what specific inhalants he has abused as well as how often, how much, and why. They also will examine the patient's behavioral and emotional patterns and talk to his family. They will draw and examine his blood to determine the levels of toxins in his body. They might also examine and/or run tests on his heart, liver, kidneys, lungs, eyes, ears, central nervous system, and/or other parts of his body. Medical staff will run neurological and cognitive tests to determine the extent of any brain damage.

If the side effects of inhalant abuse are significant, the patient will begin a rehabilitation program. She may have to stay at a rehab facility or partake in the program as an outpatient. Rehab programs for inhalant abusers are generally much longer than those for abusers of other drugs. They often last three or four months. One reason for the lengthy program is that the detoxification process (waiting for the body to rid itself of most of its toxins) could last several weeks.

During rehab, the patient might be treated by a physician for physical ailments and/or a psychiatrist for psychological damage. Depending on her condition, the patient may have to undergo physical therapy. While in rehab, she will talk with a counselor and perhaps another patient, someone who will act as a positive role model. Meanwhile, the patient and her family will be educated about the dangers of inhalants. The family will be urged to rid the home of inhalants and to support the patient as much as possible.

Even after rehab, the patient may need to paricipitate in an aftercare program. This might include continued therapy if the

▲ Sniffing markers was another way that some young people abused inhalants.

patient has suffered permanent damage. Family members, and perhaps a school counselor, will be part of the aftercare. They will need to help the patient cope with any physical, behavioral, or emotional damage she may have suffered. They will also need to make sure she does not relapse. With proper treatment—and love and understanding—a person recovering from inhalant abuse can go on to live a fulfilling life.

Spread the Word

You now know about the potentially devastating effects of inhalants. But do your brother and sister know? What about your cousins, your friends, and all the kids in your school? You could save a life simply by informing people of the dangers of inhalants.

You can spread the word in many different ways. You can start by telling your family members, perhaps urging them to search "inhalants" on the Internet. You can write a note to your teacher, saying that inhalant awareness would be a good topic for social studies, current events, health, or science.

Perhaps you can write a brief essay about inhalants that can be read to classmates or posted in the classroom. You should also tell your teacher or art teacher about the dangers of glues, old markers, correction fluid, paint, and paint thinners. The art teacher should keep an eye out for sniffers and make sure the classroom is well ventilated.

Think about going schoolwide with this issue. Ask if you and your friends can design a poster about inhalant dangers that can be hung in your school's halls. Consider writing a letter to your principal, the PTA, or the local school board urging them to educate students about inhalant abuse.

If you are in scouting, camps, or other social clubs, tell your group leader about inhalants. He or she might want to discuss the topic at the next meeting. Write a letter to the editors of your local newspaper that the third week in March is National

Inhalants & Poisons Awareness Week. At that time, they may want to print a story about this highly important topic.

▷ Make a Personal Commitment

Above all, you yourself need to refrain from inhaling toxic chemicals. Realize that sniffing invisible fumes is not much different from drinking poison out of a bottle. Weigh the pros and cons: Is a cheap high worth potential brain damage, lifelong suffering, or even death?

If you have a problem with inhalants, you must summon the courage to tell someone about it. If it is too difficult for you to discuss it in person, write an e-mail to an adult whom you trust or contact helpful organizations.

Many young people feel like they do not belong. Some feel so low that they do not care about abusing their bodies or ruining their lives. A troubled woman named Katie said, "I knew I'd got

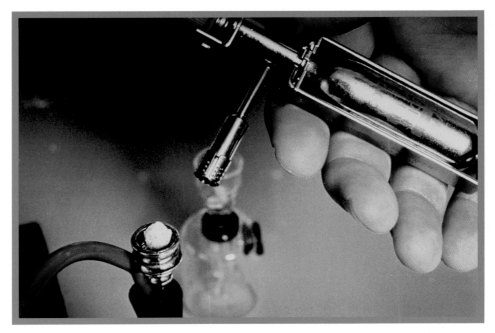

△ Some people convert tools or laboratory equipment into devices that can be used to ingest toxic chemicals.

to the end of the road when I was doing spray paint. I was pretty desperate. I didn't do it because I sort of wanted the particular high it gave me. I just did it 'cause I was desperate to escape . . ."[3]

If you feel this way—if you feel like nothing in life matters anymore—consider this: Teenage outcasts often emerge as society's freshest thinkers and greatest artists. Steven Spielberg, for example, never fit in as a teenager in Arizona. Instead of indulging in drugs, he immersed himself in filmmaking and became a successful director. You, too, have the potential to live a rich and fulfilling life if you remain drug free.

Instead of inhalants, consider life's many natural highs: swimming, skiing, hiking, and biking. You can go dancing, to the movies, or to sporting events. You can perhaps join a club or play a team sport. Or you can express yourself through music, writing, acting, or anything else of interest.

Erin chose the wrong diversion. She got high by sniffing correction fluid for typewriters. "It's already damaged my lungs," she wrote. "I have asthma, and I find it hard just running now." Erin admitted that she could not stop her addiction and that she needed help. "So if any of you are considering it," she said, "it is addicting. Don't even start."[4]

◀ Asthma, a respiratory disease, is one of the many long-term side effects of inhalant abuse. People with severe asthma need to use inhalers such as this one to aid their breathing. Sadly, some inhalant abusers fill inhalers with toxic chemicals to get high.

addiction—Involuntary psychological, physical, or emotional dependence upon a substance that is known by the user to be harmful or dangerous.

anesthetic—Something that produces the loss of sensation.

aerosol—A substance dispensed from a pressurized container in the form of fine solid or liquid particles.

butane—A type of fuel that is usually obtained in a liquid form in objects such as cigarette lighters.

ethylene gas—A naturally occurring colorless and flammable gas. Different forms of ethylene are used to make products such as antifreeze and plastics.

fluorocarbon—Any chemical compound containing carbon and fluorine mostly used as a lubricant, refrigerant, or nonstick coating.

hallucination—Perception of the presence of objects that are not real or physically there.

huffing—To inhale rigorously through the mouth.

nebulizers—Small, plastic, bowl-shaped inhalers that deliver medicine in the form of a mist spray.

nitrite—A highly toxic form of nitrogen.

solvent—Something that other substances can dissolve into.

Sudden Sniffing Death Syndrome (SSDS)—When the inhalation of a chemical causes severe stress to the heart, resulting in a very irregular heartbeat, which causes a person to collapse or die.

Chapter 1. The Silent Epidemic

1. "APRC Fact Sheet: Inhalants," *Arizona Prevention Resource Center*, n.d., <http://www.azprevention.org/Downloadable_Documents/Inhalants.pdf> (June 9, 2004).

2. Cate Baily, "Inhalants," *Scholastic News*, n.d., <http://teacher.scholastic.com/scholasticnews/indepth/headsup/facts/index.asp?article=drug_inhalents> (December 5, 2003).

3. Wendy Grossman, "Huffing dangers," *Augusta Chronicle*, September 9, 1997, <http://www.augustachronicle.com/stories/090997/xtrm_huffing.html> (December 5, 2003).

4. Jaine Treadwell, "Inhalants Drug of Choice for Some Kids," *MAP Inc.*, August 9, 2003, <http://www.mapinc.org/drugnews/v03/n1207/a06.html> (December 6, 2003).

5. Wendy Grossman, "Huffing dangers," *Augusta Chronicle*, September 9, 1997, <http://www.augustachronicle.com/stories/090997/xtrm_huffing.html> (December 5, 2003).

6. "Honest Drug Abuse Information," *DrugAbuse.com*, November 27, 2002, <http://www.drugabuse.com/boards/thd2x632.shtml> (December 7, 2003).

7. Ibid.

8. "Newsletter," *Parents: The Anti-Drug*, January 1, 2003, <http://www.theantidrug.com/sharing_listening/topics.asp?topic=3&page=5> (December 7, 2003).

9. Ibid.

10. Susan Gembrowski, "Warning is sounded on 'huffing,'" *Communities Against Substance Abuse*, March 21, 2000, <http://www.drugfreesandiego.org/htm/03inf-01atc-20000321.htm> (December 7, 2003).

Chapter 2. History of Inhalants

1. "What A Gas: Part II," *History House*, n.d., <http://www.historyhouse.com/in_history/nitrous_two> (December 11, 2003).

2. George Beschner and Alfred S. Friedman, *Teen Drug Use* (Boston: D.C. Heath and Company), 1986, p. 2.

3. *National Drug Control Strategy: 2001 Annual Report* (Washington, D.C.: Office of National Drug Control Policy, 2001), p. 148.

4. Maxim W. Furek, "The Silent Killer: Inhalant Abuse," *Full Spectrum Recovery*, n.d., <http://www.fullspectrumrecovery.com/articles/uploaded/Inhalant%20.pdf> (December 10, 2003).

5. "Inhalants," *Office of National Drug Policy*, n.d., <http://www.whitehousedrugpolicy.gov/drugfact/inhalants/inhalants_b.html> (December 10, 2003).

6. Eve Bender, "Cognitive, Behavior Problems Plague Inhalant Users," *Psychiatric News*, April 18, 2003, <http://pn.psychiatryonline.org/cgi/content/full/38/8/19> (December 12, 2003).

7. Diane Stem, "Personal Testimony: Inhalants," *Parenting Is Prevention*, March 15, 2001, <http://www.parentingisprevention.org/dstem.html> (December 13, 2003).

Chapter 3. Effects of Inhalants

1. Kathleen Fackelmann, "Abuse of Inhalants a Nationwide Problem," *The Honolulu Advertiser*, March 31, 2002, <http://the.honoluluadvertiser.com/article/2002/Mar/31/oh/oh06a.html> (December 15, 2003).

2. "NIDA Joins in Recognizing National Inhalants and Poisons Awareness Week in March," *National Institute on Drug Abuse*, March 19, 2001, <http://www.nih.gov/news/pr/mar2001/march19newsscanpdf.pdf> (December 16, 2003).

3. Wendy Grossman, "Huffing dangers," *Augusta Chronicle*, September 9, 1997, <http://www.augustachronicle.com/stories/090997/xtrm_huffing.html> (December 5, 2003).

4. Jaine Treadwell, "Inhalants Drug of Choice for Some Kids," *MAP Inc.*, August 9, 2003, <http://www.mapinc.org/drugnews/v03/n1207/a06.html> (December 16, 2003).

5. Sarah MacLean, "'Just a Dirty Kind of Drug:' Young People's Perception of Chroming," *Australian Institute of Criminology*, n.d., <http://www.aic.gov.au/conferences/2003-inhalant/maclean.pdf> (December 18, 2003).

6. Wendy Grossman, "Huffing dangers."

7. Cate Baily, "Pain Meets Poison," *Scholastic News*, n.d., <http://teacher.scholastic.com/scholasticnews/indepth/headsup/story_megan.htm> (December 19, 2003).

8. "Breathing Deep . . . And Dying," *Advance for Managers of Respiratory Care*, n.d., <http://www.advanceformrc.com/common/editorial/editorial.aspx?CC=2367> (December 19, 2003).

Chapter 4. Inhalant Abuse

1. David Van Horn, "Household Inhalants Pose Danger," *healthAtoZ*, n.d., <http://www.healthatoz.com/healthatoz/Atoz/dc/caz/suba/tnsa/alert05122001.html> (December 21, 2003).

2. Jeanie Lerche Davis, "Inhalant Abuse: Growing Problem Often Starts With Very Young," *WebMD*, August 4, 2000, <http://my.webmd.com/content/article/27/1728_60099> (December 21, 2003).

3. "Nitrous and a Liquid Slide Can," *Erowid*, February 26, 2002, <http://www.erowid.org/experiences/exp.php?ID=6402> (December 21, 2003).

4. Elizabeth L. McGarvey, et al., "Adolescent Inhalant Abuse: Environments of Use," *American Journal of Drug and Alcohol Abuse*, October 1999, <http://www.findarticles.com/cf_dls/m0978/4_25/58114629/p4/article.jhtml?term=> (December 22, 2003).

5. "Inhalants," *Office of National Drug Policy*, n.d., <http://www.whitehousedrugpolicy.gov/drugfact/inhalants> (December 22, 2003).

Chapter 5. Avoiding Inhalants

1. "What's Up With Inhalants?" *Drug Enforcement Administration*, n.d., <http://www.usdoj.gov/dea/pubs/straight/inhalant.htm> (December 27, 2003).

2. Wendy Grossman, "Huffing dangers," *Augusta Chronicle*, September 9, 1997, <http://www.augustachronicle.com/stories/090997/xtrm_huffing.html> (December 5, 2003).

3. Sarah MacLean, "'Just a Dirty Kind of Drug': Young People's Perception of Chroming," *Australian Institute of Criminology*, n.d., <http://www.aic.gov.au/conferences/2003-inhalant/maclean.pdf> (December 18, 2003).

4. Arizona Foundation for Legal Services and Education, "Substances," *LawForKids.org*, October 19, 2003, <http://www.lawforkids.org/QA/substances/substances19.cfm> (December 29, 2003).

Further Reading

Babbit, Nikki. *Adolescent Drug and Alcohol Abuse: How to Spot It, Stop It, and Get Help for Your Family.* Sebastopol, Calif.: O'Reilly & Associates, Inc., 2000.

Bayer, Linda. *Inhalants.* Philadelphia, Chelsea House, 1999.

Bellenir, Karen. *Drug Information for Teens: Health Tips About the Physical and Mental Effects of Substance Abuse.* Detroit, Mich.: Omnigraphics, 2002.

Blachford, Stacey L. and Kristine Krapp, eds. *Drugs and Controlled Substances: Information for Students.* Detroit, Mich.: Thomson/Gale, 2003.

Connolly, Sean. *Inhalants.* Chicago: Heinemann Library, 2003.

Kuhn, Cynthia, et al. *Buzzed: The Straight Dope About the Most Used and Abused Drugs from Alcohol to Ecstasy.* New York: W. W. Norton & Company, Inc., 2003.

Lobo, Ingrid A. *Inhalants.* Philadelphia: Chelsea House Publishers, 2003.

————. *Just Say Know: Talking with Kids about Drugs and Alcohol.* New York: W. W. Norton & Company, Inc., 2002.

Monroe, Judy. *Inhalant Drug Dangers.* Springfield, N.J.: Enslow Publishers, Inc., 1999.

O'Donnell, Kerri. *Inhalants and Your Nasal Passages: The Incredibly Disgusting Story.* New York: The Rosen Publishing Group, Inc., 2001.

Parker, Phillip M. and James N. Parker (eds.). *The Official Patient's SourceBook on Inhalants Dependence.* San Diego: Icon Health Publications, 2002.

Sherry, Clifford. *Inhalants.* New York: The Rosen Publishing Group, Inc., 2001.

Help Lines

National Inhalant Prevention Coalition
   1–800–269–4237

NAADAC, The Association of Addiction Professionals
   1–800–548–0497

Drug & Alcohol Treatment Referral National Hotline
   1–800–662–4357

National Helplines
   1–800–HELP–111

Narcotics Anonymous
   1–818–773–9999